WHAT'S THE BEST WAY TO LIVE?

Written by Andy Steiger & Rachel MacKenzie
Illustrated by Maggie Richards

THE HUMAN PROJECT FOR Kids

Dedication

For all the children who inspired this book, may you always know you are loved and may you always seek to love God and people. Special thanks to our Korean friend Steve Kim who helped make this book great!

What's The Best Way to Live?
The Human Project for Kids

Published by Apologetics Canada Publishing
2829 Westside Place, Abbotsford, BC V2T 4W4

Printed in Canada
First Published 2022

ISBN: 978-0-9940157-6-1

INTRODUCTION

As parents, we want the best life for our children, but what does that look like? People tend to give a lot of thought on how best to invest their money, but relatively little thought on how best to invest their lives. Jesus teaches that our life is our greatest treasure, and above all, to invest it wisely. When it comes to time, children truly are the wealthy among us and in need of wise counsel as they invest their lives.

What is the best way to live? What will lead to a flourishing life both now and eternally? Jesus answered both these questions, in his life and teaching, emphasizing the value of relationship. Jesus taught us to love God and people and that this would lead to our flourishing. Have you ever noticed that people at the end of their life do not surround themselves with accomplishments or possessions but God and people? This should challenge the way we live the whole of our lives. We hope this book inspires meaningful conversations on this important topic as you teach a child that the best way to live is in right relationship with God and people.

The Human Project for Kids is a resource for families. We want to partner with you as you train your children to have a correct perspective of God, themselves, and others. This series of books is designed to engage and capture your child's attention while teaching them Biblical truths about what it means to be human, what the value of human life is, and what leads to human flourishing.

Get more info: thehumanprojectforkids.ca

This is Sunny. She lives in South Korea and loves going on adventures with her Halmeoni. Halmeoni means Grandma in Korean. It sounds like "hal-mo-knee."

Today they are going to Ocean Adventure Park. Sunny was careful to pack everything she needed.

PACKING LIST
DO NOT FORGET!!
camera
tickets
ADMIT ONE
sun
reen
backpack
water bottle
comfy shoes

Sunny wanted this to be the best day so she made a plan. That way, she knew she wouldn't miss anything.

When they arrived at the park, Sunny checked off the first item on her list.

Halmeoni was worried that they didn't have tickets yet but Sunny reminded her that mom had already bought them from the website. Sunny didn't want them to waste any time waiting in line.

Pulling out her checklist, Sunny showed Halmeoni how she had made a plan to make sure they had the best day.

BEST day EVER
OFFICIAL PLAN
SELFIE AT THE GATES
WIN A PRIZE
GET WET ON A WATER RIDE
FIND THE BEST FOOD
GET DIZZY ON A SPINNING RIDE
RIDE THE ROLLERCOASTER
S

As they walked through the entrance, Sunny noticed the biggest stuffed animals she had ever seen. Winning one of these prizes was on the top of her list.

The game was harder than she expected. Sunny was worried that if she didn't win, her day would be ruined. She took a deep breath and made her final toss.

"I won!" shouted Sunny.

They named the giant stuffy "Bubbles" and then made their way to the next stop on their great adventure.

Sunny had planned to go on the water ride early in the day so they had time to dry while the sun was hot.

"Come on, Halmeoni! We need to sit here so that we get the biggest splash!" Sunny exclaimed.

When they got off the ride, Halmeoni was wet...really wet. Surprisingly, her umbrella and poncho didn't keep her as dry as she had hoped. Sunny was worried that she might have ruined their best day.

"That was a fun ride together, Sunny. What's next?" asked Halmeoni with a smile.

Sunny was relieved that Halmeoni enjoyed the ride and was okay with being wet.

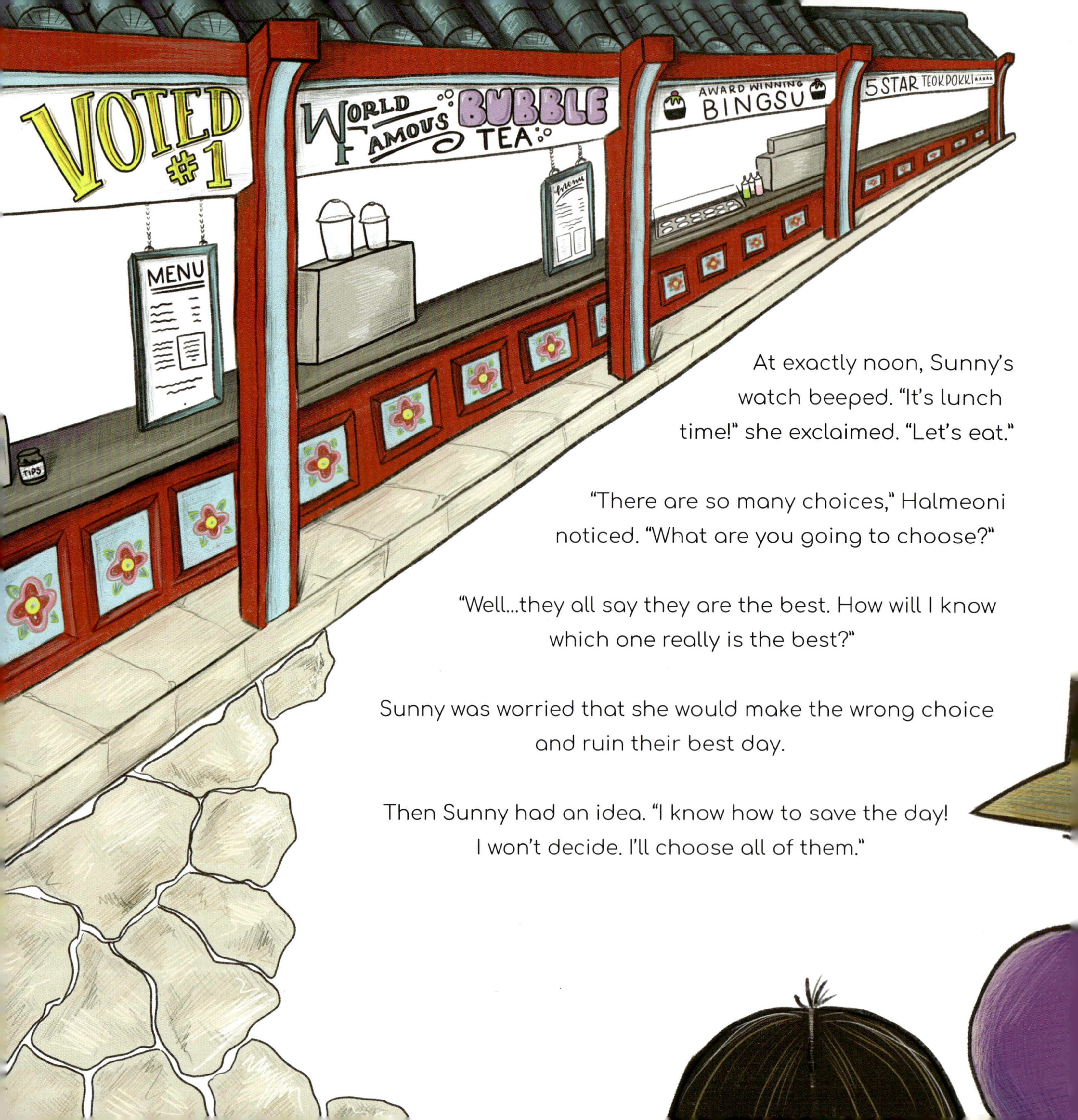

At exactly noon, Sunny's watch beeped. "It's lunch time!" she exclaimed. "Let's eat."

"There are so many choices," Halmeoni noticed. "What are you going to choose?"

"Well...they all say they are the best. How will I know which one really is the best?"

Sunny was worried that she would make the wrong choice and ruin their best day.

Then Sunny had an idea. "I know how to save the day! I won't decide. I'll choose all of them."

Not wanting Halmeoni to miss out on all the great food, Sunny offered, "Do you want to try some?"

"Thank you Sunny," Halmeoni replied, "but I'm content. I'm just happy to be having lunch together with you." It took Sunny a long time to eat all that food but she was determined to try it all.

"Which one was the best?" Halmeoni asked.

Sunny just groaned. "I don't know. I don't feel very good. Next time I'll just choose one."

After lunch, they continued to check off the items on Sunny's list, one by one. "This really is turning out to be the best day," thought Sunny.

Pulling out her list, they made their way to the ride that Sunny was most looking forward to -- the Sea Monster Coaster.

"I saved the best for last!" Sunny said excitedly.

TREASURE
HUNT
G FISH
AIN
SEA

While they waited in line, Sunny explained to Halmeoni that the *best* way to ride the rollercoaster is in the front.

Looking nervous, Halmeoni said, “But we don’t need to sit in the very front, do we?"

"Yes we do!" explained Sunny. "For this to be the best day, we need to have the perfect seat!"

With a good plan and a little bit of luck, Sunny, Halmeoni, and Bubbles took their seats in the front row.

With every click of the rollercoaster on the tracks, they made their way higher and higher until they could see the whole park. As they reached the top and were about to plunge straight down, Sunny threw her hands up in the air and ...

With a loud KERPLUNK! the ride came to a sudden stop. Halmeoni opened her eyes and asked with surprise, “Is it over?”

“No. We didn’t go anywhere yet!” replied Sunny. “The ride is stuck!”

As Sunny looked around, she realized that she could not fix this problem. Soon, her fear was confirmed, when over the loudspeaker it was announced that the ride was broken.

“Oh no!” gasped Sunny.

“I’m sure they can fix it,” Halmeoni said, as she squeezed Sunny’s hand.

“I’m worried that our best day is ruined!” Sunny cried.

“Why can’t this still be a great day?” Halmeoni asked Sunny.

“Because everything needs to be perfect,” she said, “and the ride breaking down is not a part of my plan.”

“I don’t think our day is ruined,” Halmeoni said.

“You don’t? What if we’re stuck here the rest of the day?”

FLYING FISH
TRAIN
GET WET ON A
WATER RIDE
ASURE
UNT
OC
PL

"I would rather be on a broken ride with you all day, than on a working one alone," Halmeoni said.

Sunny was shocked. She had never thought about that before. "Would this have been the best day if I was by myself?" she wondered.

"I've had lots of adventures where things have gone wrong. Some of them are my favourite memories," Halmeoni continued.

"How could this become a favourite memory if everything doesn't go perfectly?" Sunny asked.

"My life has had lots of best days and they were all because of who I was with, not because everything went perfectly," Halmeoni answered.

Sunny was starting to understand. "So, you're still having a good day because you're with me?"

"Any day I spend with you is a great day."

Sunny looked thoughtfully down at the adventure park. She pulled out her list and noticed her plan was all about what she was doing and not who she was with. Sunny imagined what her day would have been like without Halmeoni.

"You're right," she realized. "I could do everything on my list but it wouldn't be the best day without you."

Pointing down from the rollercoaster, Halmeoni said, “Look at everyone in this adventure park. Do you see anyone not having a good day?”

Sunny looked around and said, “Yeah, I see some people having a bad day.”

“Often when something goes wrong, we only see the problem right in front of us. What are they *not* seeing?” Halmeoni asked.

“The big picture?” Sunny guessed.

“You’re right,” Halmeoni said. “It looks like they’ve forgotten the people around them. They let their problem stop them from enjoying who they are with.”

Sunny began to think about that and said, "Halmeoni, you must have a lot of bad days."

Halmeoni was surprised. "Why do you think that?"

"When I'm at school and Mom and Dad are at work, you are at home all alone."

Halmeoni laughed, "I do have friends besides our family, Sunny. But more importantly, I have Someone who is always with me."

"You do? You're never alone?" Sunny asked.

"Sunny, when I pray, I'm reminded that God is always with me. The Bible teaches that my best days are when I live this adventure of life with God."

"God wants you to have not only the best day but the best life!"

"Really?" Sunny asked, "Then why are we stuck on this rollercoaster?"

YOU WILL SHOW ME THE WAY OF LIFE, GRANTING ME THE JOY OF YOUR PRESENCE AND THE PLEASURE OF LIVING WITH YOU FOREVER
PSALM 16:11 (NLT)

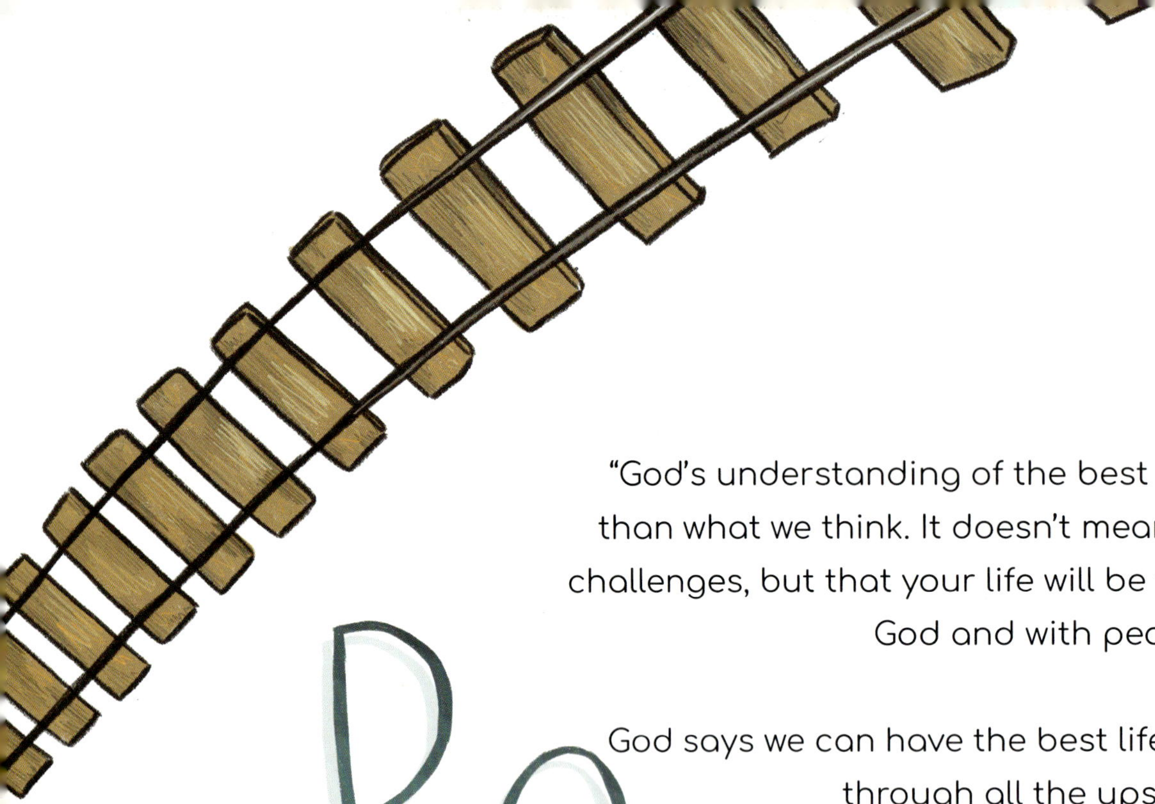

"God's understanding of the best life is often different than what we think. It doesn't mean that you won't have challenges, but that your life will be full of relationship with God and with people.

God says we can have the best life when we follow Him through all the ups and...

DOWNS!

Halmeoni gasped as the rollercoaster suddenly began working again. Grabbing Sunny's hand they raised their arms and screamed together as they twisted and loop-de-looped through the air.

"That was so much fun!" Sunny yelled as the ride came to a stop. "I'm so glad we went on that ride together!"

"Even though it broke down?" Halmeoni asked.

"We did get to spend more time together and being with you is better than a perfect ride."

As Sunny and Halmeoni walked through the park, Sunny thought about their conversation at the top of the rollercoaster. She understood that being together is what made this a great day but she was still a little puzzled.

"What about when I'm not with you, Halmeoni? How do I have a relationship with God like you do?"

"The way to have a relationship with God is through Jesus," Halmeoni replied. "He is like a map who shows us the way to God. He teaches us the best way to live with God and each other."

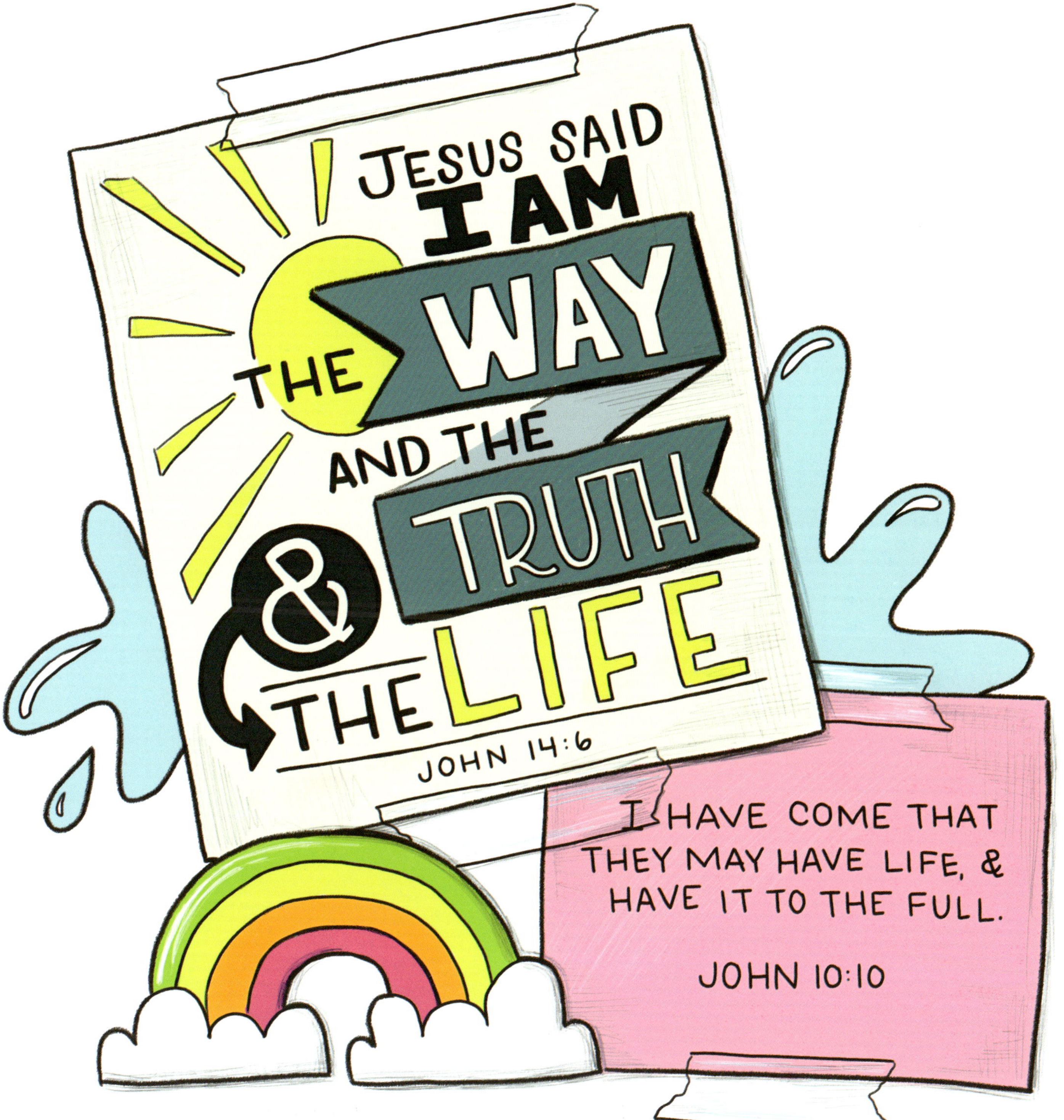
JESUS SAID
I AM
THE WAY
AND THE
TRUTH
&
THE LIFE
JOHN 14:6
I HAVE COME THAT THEY MAY HAVE LIFE, & HAVE IT TO THE FULL.
JOHN 10:10

BEST DAY EVER!!

"When we read the Bible we can see the way Jesus lived and what He taught," Halmeoni continued.

"The Bible teaches that just like us, Jesus had challenges. But unlike us, He never stopped loving God and people in both the good times and the bad. Even when things break down in our life, like the rollercoaster, Jesus teaches us not to lose sight of the big picture: living together with God."

As they were leaving the park, Sunny asked, "So, with Jesus, I can have the best life?"

"Exactly," Halmeoni replied. "Through Jesus you can have a relationship with God. He wants to teach you how to love God and people through the good and bad. As you learn to love God, He teaches you to love people. Investing in these relationships is the best way to live."

As Sunny got on the scooter and wrapped her arms around Halmeoni, she thought -- "This really was the best day ever!"

KEEP LEARNING

1. At the beginning, what did Sunny think she needed to have the best day?

2. Do you have a memory of a best day that didn't go perfectly?

3. How did Sunny's thinking about what was needed for the best day change throughout the story?

4. What evidence was there that Halmeoni valued relationship over a perfect day?

5. Share some examples of how Jesus loved God and people in the Bible. What can we learn from His example?

6. Do you have a relationship with God through Jesus? If not, the person reading this book with you would love to help you start.